CHANGING WORLD
KENYA

CHANGING WORLD

KENYA

Tish Farrell

ARCTURUS

Reprinted in 2013
This edition first published in 2010 by Arcturus Publishing
Distributed by Black Rabbit Books
P.O. Box 3263
Mankato
Minnesota MN 56002

Copyright © 2010 Arcturus Publishing Limited

Printed in The United States of America

Library of Congress Cataloging-in-Publication Data

Farrell, Tish.
  Kenya / Tish Farrell.
      p. cm. -- (Changing world)
  Includes index.
  ISBN 978-1-84837-643-4 (library bound)
  I. Kenya--Juvenile literature. I. Title.

  DT433.522.F34 2011
  967.62--dc22

                              2009051186

Series concept: Alex Woolf
Editor: Jacqueline McCann
Designer: Ian Winton
Maps and charts: Stefan Chabluk
Picture researcher: Jacqueline McCann

Picture credits:
Chris Fairclough/Discovery Photo Library: 21, 23, 28, 34.
Corbis: title page and 6 (John Warburton Lee), 12 (Paul Souders), 15 (Bettman), 18 (Louise Gubb),
21 (Wendy Stone), 22 (Buddy Mays), 25 (Amanda Coster), 26 (Stephen Morrison/EPA), 27 (EPA/Standard RM),
36 (Wendy Stone), 38 (Radu Sigheti), 39 (Gideon Mendel), 40 (Anthony Njuguna), 41 (Peter Turnley),
42 (Wendy Stone).
Getty: cover right (Travel Ink), 9 (Robert Harding), 11 (Julia Bayne), 13 (Travel Ink), 14 (Paul Thompson/FPG/Stringer),
16 (Central Press), 17 (Alexander Joe), 19 (Paula Bronstein), 20 (Jeff Rotman), 30 (Jason LaVeris), 31 (Stringer),
32 (Paul Kenward), 35 (Joseph Van Os), 37 (Bobby Haas), 43 (Jamie Squire).
Science Photo Library: cover left and 8 (Art Wolfe), 10 (Philippe Plailly/Eurelios), 24 (Jason Kelvin).

Cover captions:
Left: Masai tribeswomen from Kenya.
Right: High-angle view over Nairobi.

ISBN: 978-1-84837-643-4
SL001313US
Supplier 02, Date 0912, Print Run 2288

Contents

CHAPTER 1

Introduction

Kenya, in East Africa, is a land of contrasts, from its tropical Indian Ocean coast to the glaciers of Mount Kenya. It lies on the equator and is bisected by the Great Rift Valley. Mombasa, the main port, is hot and humid, with temperatures around 86 degrees Fahrenheit, F (30 degrees Celcius, C). The capital, Nairobi, is 248 miles (400 kilometers, km) inland and nearly 6,560 feet (2,000 meters, m) higher. It has warm days, around 75°F (24°C), and cool nights of 50 to 57°F (10 to 14°C). From Nairobi, the rift escarpments rise to over 9,840 feet (3,000 m), through forested slopes and bamboo thickets to frosty moorlands. Higher still, at over 16,400 feet (5,000 m), rises Mount Kenya. North and east of there, the land is bush country turning to desert.

COMPARING COUNTRIES: HOW BIG IS KENYA?

Kenya is smaller than Texas but more than twice the size of the United Kingdom (UK).

Area in square miles (square kilometers)

Texas, US	271,144 (695,241)
Kenya	227,234 (582,650)
France	213,342 (547,030)
UK	95,480 (244,820)
Switzerland	16,103 (41,290)

Source: CIA *World Factbook*, 2009

On the wild side

Kenya's wildlife reserves and fine beaches attract up to 1 million foreign tourists each year. Tourism and horticulture exports provide Kenya's main income. The Maasai Mara reserve is famous for its great wildebeest migrations, but wildlife also

Mount Kenya, Kenya's tallest mountain, dominates the skyline of the upland plains. By contrast, the lowland plains are much hotter and drier, with only occasional trees. Thorn scrub grassland is typical of much of the country's semi-arid areas.

The Great Rift Valley creates much of Kenya's geographical variety. Farming is concentrated on either side of the valley in two densely inhabited zones that get plenty of rainfall. The east and north are arid and support only small numbers of nomadic herders.

roams freely outside the parks. Local people often resent the Kenya Wildlife Service for protecting wildlife at the expense of people who need the land.

Fertile highlands

Only 15 percent of Kenya's arable land is sufficiently fertile and gets enough rainfall to sustain agriculture. The best land is in the central and western highlands, where most people live. Here the climate suits wheat farming and crops such as flowers, coffee, and tea. Most farms are small and mainly grow maize, kale, squash, beans, sweet potatoes, and some tomatoes. Goats and chickens are kept for meat, but due to a shortage of land, dairy cattle are usually "zero grazed" which means they are kept in pens and fodder is brought to them.

Waiting for rain

Most farmers rely on two rainy seasons brought by the Indian Ocean's monsoon winds: the long rains planting season from March to May and the short rains in November and December. Everyone depends on lakes and rivers for drinking, cooking, and washing water. These lakes and rivers are fed by Kenya's five "water towers"—the highland forests of Mount Kenya, Aberdares, Mau, the Cherangani Hills, and Mount Elgon. These vital areas are increasingly threatened by illegal logging or felling trees for cooking fuel. In recent years, global climate change has brought severe drought in arid areas and flooding in the highlands.

SUDAN

ETHIOPIA

UGANDA

Lake
Turkana

GREAT RIFT VALLEY

KENYA

SOMALIA

Eldoret

Meru

Equator

Kisumu

Nakuru

ABERDARES

△Mount Kenya

Nyeri

Tana River

Lake
Victoria

MAU

Athi River

Nairobi

Machakos

Lamu Island

Galana River

TANZANIA

N

INDIAN

OCEAN

Key
■ Capital city
● Other towns
△ Mountains
▨ Cultivated areas
▨ Forested areas
▨ Game parks

Mombasa

Pemba

Zanzibar

Multicultural Kenya

Kenya has more than 40 ethnic communities with three main language groups: Cushites, Nilotes, and Bantus. Cushite speakers include the nomadic Somali camel herders living in the dry northeast. The cattle-owning Maasai and Luo fishermen-farmers of Lake Victoria are Nilotes. The Kikuyu, Luhya, and Akamba belong to the biggest language group, the Bantu-speaking farmers. The Swahili are a mix of Bantu and Arab peoples who live on the coast. There are small numbers of Europeans, Asians, and Arabs. Kenya also provides sanctuary for many refugees from neighboring Somalia, Sudan, and Uganda.

The Maasai cattle herders live by age-old traditions and wear their eye-catching tribal dress. Most urban Kenyans, however, have adopted European ways of life.

Town and country living

Many Kenyan families own small farms in the rural highlands that they regard as ancestral land. These days, such plots may be too small or overworked to support a family, so husbands seek paid employment in the towns while their wives stay on the farm with the children. Migrant workers may return home only once or twice a year. They grow used to town ways and gradually bring back those ways to up-country areas. Rural communities that are close to urban centers tend to be the most Westernized and their children the best educated. In remote areas, people such as the Maasai and Turkana still proudly keep their traditional dress and customs.

The majority of Kenya's population are Bantu-speaking farming communities and include the Kikuyu of Central Province, the Luhya of Western Province, and the Akamba of Eastern Province. The Luo from Lake Victoria are the largest Nilotic-speaking group.

Main ethnic groups

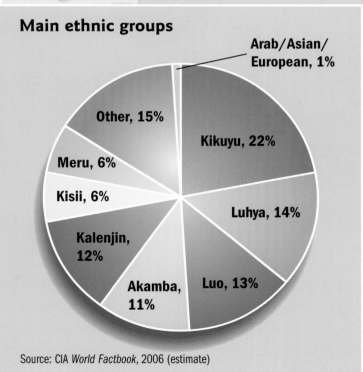

Arab/Asian/European, 1%
Other, 15%
Kikuyu, 22%
Meru, 6%
Kisii, 6%
Luhya, 14%
Kalenjin, 12%
Akamba, 11%
Luo, 13%

Source: CIA *World Factbook*, 2006 (estimate)

Urban centers

Kenya's three key urban centers are linked by air, rail, and road. Mombasa, the main seaport, has a long mercantile history and today is the trading hub for East and Central Africa. Its population is mainly Muslim. Nairobi, the capital city, is the region's financial center. Founded in 1900, when the British were building the Uganda Railway, it is predominantly Christian although multicultural in outlook. Until independence in 1963, the town existed to serve European settlers, and Africans were subjected to segregation laws. Now it is a multinational center for banks, tourist hotels, casinos, shopping malls, and manufacturing plants. It hosts a large diplomatic community and many international aid agencies. Kenya's educated elite works in Nairobi as lawyers, bankers, teachers, doctors, and information technology specialists. Thousands of migrant workers are employed as security guards, store clerks, house servants, company drivers, hotel waiters, cleaners, and porters. They rent rooms in the slums and send most of their earnings back to their rural homes. On Lake Victoria, the small town of Kisumu provides an inland port with links to neighboring Tanzania, Uganda, and countries of the Great Lakes region. It is the main trading center for local Luo and Luhya people.

Of the 2 million Kenyans in waged employment, 75 percent work in agriculture while 25 percent have jobs in industry and services.

Nairobi sprang up from a few railway workers' sheds left behind after the building of the Uganda Railway. Today, it is the financial hub of East Africa and regional headquarters for many international companies.

CHAPTER 2

History

Kenya's history goes back to the time when our pre-human ancestors roamed the Great Rift Valley. One of the earliest Kenyan fossils is a 6-million-year-old hominid (ape-man) from the Lake Baringo district. The oldest human settlement is at Olorgesaillie (43 miles, or 70 km, southwest of Nairobi), where archaeologists have

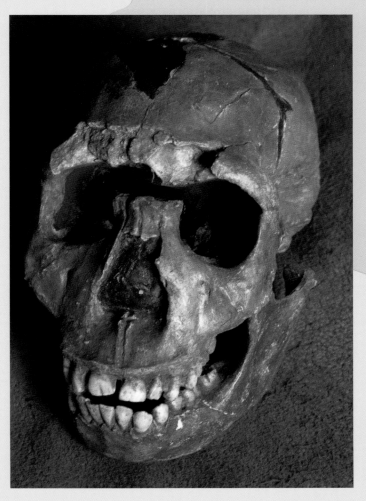

FOCUS: TURKANA BOY

In 1984, Kenyan researcher Kamoya Kimeu found the fossil skeleton of a boy near Lake Turkana, northern Kenya, who lived 1.6 million years ago. Scientists have classified him as our pre-human ancestor *Homo erectus* or *Homo ergaster*. The shape of the pelvic bones shows he was male. Presence of adult teeth suggests he was nine to 12 years old. His brain size was 49 cubic inches (880 cubic centimeters, cc) (a modern human's adult brain is 82 cubic inches, or 1,350 cc). But at five feet, two inches (160 centimeters, cm), he was surprisingly tall. His remains, along with many important fossil finds, are studied and displayed at Nairobi's National Museum, a world center for paleontological research.

found many stone tools. The incisions on bones of an extinct elephant species also found there show that these early people were butchering meat. Kenya's first human inhabitants were hunter-gatherers who probably lived in small nomadic groups. They roamed Kenya's game-rich plains from about 1 million years ago.

This photograph shows the fossilized skull of Turkana Boy, one of the oldest examples of our pre-human ancestors, *Homo erectus*. His recovered skeleton is almost complete and continues to be studied by Kenyan scientists at Nairobi's National Museum.

Herders and farmers

About 4,000 years ago, Cushitic-speaking nomads from the Horn of Africa began to arrive in Kenya, followed by Nilotic nomads from Sudan. These nomads lived by keeping herds of cattle, goats, and sheep. Then, 2,000 years ago, the first iron-working Bantu farmers began to settle in western and coastal Kenya. Over the next 1,500 years, other, similar groups arrived and staked out clan territories. Today, the descendants of all these invaders make up Kenya's diverse communities.

The land of Zanj

The Bantu coastal settlers were influenced by Arab culture. By 100 CE, Arab merchant seafarers were visiting East Africa's shores. The Arabs called Africa "Zanj" and their sailing dhows came and went with the monsoon winds. A sailor's log from these times tells us the Arabs traded daggers, glass, and wheat for African ivory, rhino horn, tortoiseshell, and coconut oil.

Lamu Old Town is one of Kenya's best-preserved Swahili towns and has been lived in for 700 years. Once a rich settlement dependent on the Arab dhow trade, it now relies on tourism for its income. In 2001, it was named a World Heritage City.

Birth of the Swahili

Many Arab merchants intermarried with the coastal Bantu, giving rise to the Swahili people. Their language, Kiswahili, a fusion of Bantu and Arabic, became the language of trade throughout East Africa. Today, it is Kenya's national language, along with English, and it is spoken in neighboring Tanzania and Uganda. The Swahili people adopted Islam and became successful traders, acting as middlemen between inland tribes and the visiting Arab dhow captains. By the eighth century, they were building fine coral-stone towns at Mombasa, Manda, Malindi, and Lamu. Each had its own sultan, and the townspeople displayed their wealth by wearing exotic silks and jewels from the Orient.

Invaders, rogue traders, slavers

In 1498, Portuguese sailor and explorer Vasco da Gama stopped at Mombasa and Malindi on his voyage around Africa. His arrival heralded two centuries of ruthless Portuguese oppression for the Swahili. The invaders built forts on the Kenyan coast, and it was not until 1698 that the Omani of coastal Arabia finally ousted them. Omani sultans then ruled the Swahili coast until the arrival of the British in the nineteenth century. The Omani were slave traders. They also needed slaves to work on their new clove plantations on the island of Zanzibar, not far off Kenya's coast. Cloves and slaves made the Omani very rich, and in 1840, Sultan Seyyid Said moved his court from Oman to Zanzibar to oversee his growing commercial empire.

Inland Kenya

During this time, the lives of Kenya's inland tribes probably changed very little. Nomadic herders followed seasonal routes searching for water and fresh pasture. Sometimes they raided other tribes

The Slave Market Memorial on Zanzibar marks the site where mainland Africans were sold as slaves. In 1866 alone, 20,000 slaves were traded at the market. It only closed in 1873, after the British Consul on Zanzibar threatened to blockade the island.

for their herds. Farmers such as the Kikuyu lived in the forest margins, tending gardens of millet, sugarcane, and sweet potatoes. They traded surplus food with the Maasai and later supplied

CASE STUDY: THE SLAVE ROAD

The rise of the Swahili states brought new goods to inland tribes, who exchanged their ivory and animal skins for cloth, pottery, wire, and beads. At first, the coastal Bantu controlled this market, but by the mid-nineteenth century, Swahili merchants were leading caravans into the interior, creating a 682-mile (1,100-km) footpath up the Rift Valley to present-day Uganda. Pack animals could not be used because of the deadly tsetse flies, so merchants used slaves to carry food and trade goods. On the return journey, fresh slaves carried new supplies of ivory tusks back to the coast.

the Swahili trading caravans. For the Kikuyu, making a living, conducting important rites relating to birth, initiation into adulthood, marriage and death, training young warriors, and praying to God and the ancestors were their concerns. When new land was needed, they went in search of it. Sometimes this led to warfare, but in peacetime, the tribes traded and intermarried.

British interest and exploration

From the early nineteenth century, the British navy patrolled East African waters in an attempt to stop the slave trade. In 1845, they finally persuaded the Sultan of Zanzibar to limit his slaving activities, but by then, Europe's rulers were more interested in Africa's interior, both in its presumed riches and finding the source of the Nile River. So began the era of exploration. The great explorers, Richard Burton and John Speke, David Livingstone, and Henry Stanley all set off from Zanzibar, relying on the Swahili slavers' expertise to equip their expeditions into Africa's interior.

Mombasa's Fort Jesus is one of several Indian Ocean garrisons built by the Portuguese in their attempt to control Far East trade. They occupied it from 1593 until a terrible siege of 1698, when it fell to the sultans of Oman.

Scramble for Africa

In the 1880s, Britain and Germany vied for East African territory. Britain feared that if Germany claimed Uganda, it could dam the Nile and cut off Egypt's water supply. This would break Britain's hold on the Suez Canal and threaten its trade with India. By 1890, Germany settled for Tanganyika (now Tanzania), while Britain took control of Zanzibar and the Kenyan mainland from Mombasa to Uganda. The new claims were mapped and boundaries drawn where no boundaries had ever been. To secure its position, Britain built a railway from Mombasa to Lake Victoria. In 1895, the territory was called British East Africa and declared a British protectorate.

Invasion

Far from protecting its new African subjects, Britain used military force to secure the proposed line of rail through tribal territories. Small forts were built at intervals, and these relied on food from the Bantu farmers. When farmers would not trade, supplies were taken by force. Once the railway was under way, European settlers began to arrive. They wanted large areas of fertile land to develop into farms, and they expected the Africans to work for them. For the next 60 years, Britain advertised for settlers to take up farming in Kenya's fertile highlands. The government needed valuable cash crops such as tea and coffee; there was an expensive railway to pay for. But success depended on cheap, local labor. Could the natives be made to work for the new settlers?

In 1865, work began on the 599-mile (966-km) Uganda Railway. It reached Lake Victoria in 1901. The British shipped 30,000 workers from India to help with construction. Hundreds died from malaria or attacks by lions. The railway became known as the Lunatic Line.

Going on safari was a popular pursuit for wealthy, adventurous Europeans in the 1920s. Here, pioneer wildlife photographer Osa Johnson shows village women how to apply makeup. Europeans generally believed it was good for Africans to learn their ways.

Colonial rule

Under British rule, native peoples found their lives and land were no longer their own. From 1905, boundaries were drawn around the land they

FOCUS: WHITE HIGHLANDS

Early settlers included aristocrats such as Lord Delamere, whose descendants still farm a ranch in the Rift Valley today. Others were veteran army officers. Missionaries settled among the African tribes to convert them to Christianity. Government administrators came to manage the protectorate, making their base in the new railway town of Nairobi. The fertile "White Highlands" of Central Province were designated for white settlement only. Some of this land belonged to the Kikuyu people, thus sowing the seeds for the 1950s Mau Mau uprising (see page 17).

occupied, which was called tribal reserves. The country was divided into seven provinces and run byprovincial and district commissioners. District officers, assisted by native policemen called *askaris*, oversaw tax collection, disease and wildlife control, and administered law and order. Chiefs and headmen were appointed to manage the natives, including gathering taxes and raising labor gangs. These men were often misfits and outsiders who exploited their power and created wealthy dynasties. This new system undermined the traditional democratic system of law and order run by councils of elders.

African grievance

In 1920, British East Africa became a Crown Colony and was called Kenya. Many more European settlers arrived on the British government's "soldier-settler" scheme, which allowed them to buy farmland cheaply. The settlers wanted plenty of African labor. But by now, many Africans were angry that they were being forced to leave their farms to work. The Kikuyu of Central Province and the Luo in west Kenya began to form political associations in a bid to have the colonial government address their grievances over land, taxation, and lack of freedom.

Colonial force

Africans did not use money before the British arrived. To force them into waged labor, the administration introduced hut and poll taxes. In 1919, all males over the age of 16 had to register for work and carry the despised *kipande* passbook that listed their employment details. During both world wars, thousands of young men were conscripted into the British forces and died without thanks. After World War II, African veterans saw white officers receive large farms under the "soldier-settler" scheme while they had to return to overcrowded reserves where there was insufficient

Jomo Kenyatta was Kenya's first president. In 1952, he was wrongly accused of masterminding the Mau Mau movement and detained until 1961. Once in power, he tried to build unity between Africans and Europeans.

land to allow them to marry and raise families. This, along with the lack of training opportunities, became a source of fury and shame.

CASE STUDY: MAU MAU AND THE EMERGENCY YEARS, 1952–56

By 1952, African resentment had turned to revolt and the Mau Mau uprising began. Freedom fighters, mostly Kikuyus, conducted a guerrilla war from the forests of Aberdares and Mount Kenya. Civilian Kikuyus swore oaths of support. The British called a state of emergency and Mau Mau suspects were sent to detention camps. While the British air force bombed the forests, 1 million Kikuyu women and children were sent to fenced camps overseen by Kikuyu Home Guards. In 1956, British official figures recorded 11,000 freedom fighters killed, 1,000 hanged, and over 80,000 detained. British forces lost fewer than 200 men, and 32 settlers were killed.

Uhuru—independence

During the emergency years, from 1952–56, there was outrage in Britain at the way Africans were treated, and despite fierce settler opposition, in 1963, the British government finally granted Kenya its independence. In 1964, Jomo Kenyatta, a Kikuyu leader whom the British had detained in 1952, became president. Many settlers left, fearing African revenge. But Kenyatta set out to create a unity that included all races. His slogan was "*Harambee*," Kiswahili for "all pull together," and for a time, there was new prosperity in Kenya.

New elite

Kenyatta ruled until his death in 1978. His successor, Daniel arap Moi, a Kalenjin, stayed in power for 24 years. Both presidents abused their power. Members of their respective Kikuyu and Kalenjin elites helped themselves to large farms and the nation's wealth, while the poor saw little lasting benefit from independence. Moi's despotic regime ended in 2002, when Mwai Kibaki and his National Rainbow Coalition party won the election, and again for a short time, Kenyans looked forward to real freedom and democracy.

Daniel arap Moi followed Kenyatta's lead as president, using power to enrich his family and political supporters. His repressive regime opposed multiparty democracy.

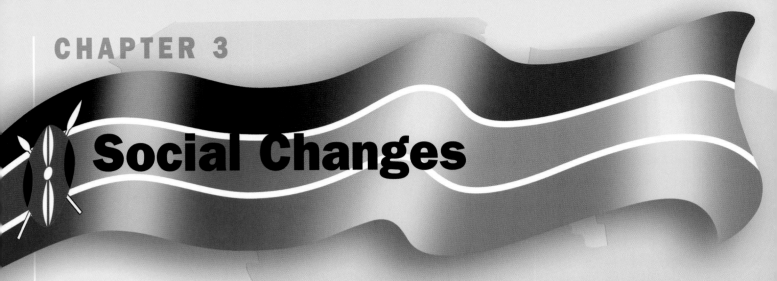

CHAPTER 3

Social Changes

In little over 100 years, Kenyan society has expanded from small-scale village life without writing, money, or complex technology to high-tech city living. Tribes most affected by European occupation, such as the Kikuyu and Luo, were quick to take up British education. However, during colonial times, the only schools available to them were run by European missionaries. In return for a basic education, Africans were obliged to give up traditional beliefs for Christianity. Today, most Kenyans are Christian and church membership is an important part of their lives.

FOCUS: TRADITIONAL BELIEFS

In the past, every community had complex spiritual beliefs. Sacred groves or rocks were the equivalent of churches, where prayers and offerings were made both to ancestors and to the creator. Most believed in a supreme being. The Luo creator is called Were or Nyasaye. The Akamba use the name Mulungu. The coastal Bantu still have their sacred forest *kayas*, or sanctuaries, and in other communities, too, older beliefs persist alongside orthodox faiths.

Young people also learn about the West from state education, movies, television, and the Internet. Urban middle-class children speak the two national languages, English and Kiswahili, but may not know their rural grandparents' language. Increasingly, the countryside and its ways may seem strange to the town child.

Old and new

In times of trouble, old customs often come to the fore. If the rains fail, villagers may still call on the rainmaker. Along the coast, where Islam predominates, there are spirit mediums

Many Kenyans still hold traditional ceremonies to mark the initiation of boys and girls into adulthood. Here, a warrior in a nomadic community blows a horn at a ceremony that marks the transition of boys to young warriors, or *moran*.

Members of the African Israel Church Nineveh spend their Sunday meetings singing, marching, and running. They are one of several independent African churches in Kenya that have adapted orthodox faiths to include many of their traditional beliefs.

who invoke the help of ancestors in times of crisis. Some Kenyans, who wish to keep their customs of polygamy (having more than one wife) and initiation, belong to independent churches. Kenya's earliest African independent church, the Nomiyo Luo Church, was founded in 1914 by Yohana Owalo.

Ancestors

Many Kenyans honor their ancestors by naming children after them or by making offerings at ceremonies. Some believe that the souls of dead family members occupy a parallel reality close to that of the living. For this reason, Kenyans prefer to be buried on clan land, referred to as ancestral land, to be close to their living family.

Rites of passage

Today, it is mostly the rural clan elders who remember the traditional customs relating to important family events of birth, initiation, marriage, and death. Younger, educated clan members bow to their opinion no matter how Westernized their town lives may be. If a Kenyan dies in town, his family will transport his body back to the rural homeland, where a customary funeral will be held. Urban dwellers also take their teenage boys back to the rural homeland for the circumcision ceremonies that initiate them into manhood, although these days the actual surgery may be done at a clinic rather than by a traditional surgeon.

Family life

While Europeans focus their resources on the nuclear family (parents and children), African life revolves around the extended family (aunts, uncles, cousins, half siblings, and stepmothers). In the past, men commonly had more than one wife, and this custom still persists. Each wife had her own house in her husband's compound, where she brought up the children. The first wife had seniority, but they all shared household tasks: fetching water, farm work, and pounding grain. When a husband died, one of his brothers would "inherit" the widow and his brother's children. Today, many Kenyan widows rebel against this, believing the custom to be outdated since they can take care of themselves.

Farming timebomb

When the British confined African farmers to tribal reserves, it had unfortunate consequences that remain unresolved to this day. Continuous grazing and cultivation reduced the fertility of the

FOCUS: TRIBE, CLAN, AND LINEAGE— WHAT ARE THEY?

A tribe is an ethnic community that shares common customs and language. It comprises clans whose members claim a distant, common ancestor. A clan consists of several family units who also claim a common ancestor. Each family group is a lineage, and this relates to the way goods or land are inherited, usually from fathers to sons. In the past, when a lineage grew too large, some of the sons would take their families to a new territory. This was one of the ways that Africa was settled before the Europeans arrived.

land. Removing tree cover for firewood or to create fields caused soil loss. The reserves had defined boundaries, so the repeated division of family plots passed from fathers to sons left people with farms too small to live off. All the land outside the reserves belonged to the British Crown or to settlers. After independence, the situation did not change for most people. Some still occupy the same impoverished ancestral land

The Elmolo, Kenya's smallest ethnic community, live in the harsh, hot north on Lake Turkana's shores. Their remote location means that the modern world has had little impact on them. They live by fishing for giant Nile perch.

Nairobi's shantytowns house over 2 million people. Housemaids, drivers, guards, laborers, and small traders with their families all rent houses there. Water, electricity, and sanitation are in short supply.

price, to the bride's family. Marriage unites two lineages, and payment of goats, cattle, or other goods cements this important social contract for the couple and their families. However, many Kenyan couples cannot afford the bride price, and in towns, where there are no elders to disapprove, young people often set up home and start families without marrying. When relationships break down, mothers may be left with children they cannot support. New partners may reject the children of previous relationships, and these children often end up living on the streets, where they are prey to violence, drug abuse, and sexual exploitation. For children to be lost from clan care in this way would not have been acceptable in pre-colonial times.

today. They cannot afford to buy more land, so husbands must leave to earn money to pay school fees and medical bills or to build a better house.

Bride price

Today, even among the educated elite, a traditional marriage will follow an official ceremony and include the payment of a dowry, or bride

A Christian "white wedding" followed by a traditional bride-price-paying party is the commonest form of marriage in Kenya. There is also now a growing demand for simple civil ceremonies with no bride price.

21

Elite living

The divide between Kenya's rich and poor is most striking in Nairobi. The wealthiest classes (Kenyan-Asian entrepreneurs, government ministers, aid workers, and diplomats) live in tree-lined avenues in the city suburbs. Homes are large, with servants' quarters, and grounds are surrounded by security fences. Rich families may employ a cook, maids, gardener, and driver. They bypass run-down public utilities by buying private services, from garbage collection to security guards. They spend their leisure time in expensive shopping malls and at country clubs that have facilities for golf, cricket, polo, and sailing. Weekends at luxury safari camps and beach hotels are only a short plane ride away.

The professionals

The middle classes live mostly in towns on suburban estates. Their homes and lifestyles are European in outlook. If both husbands and wives work, they will employ a maid, sometimes a relative, to look after the children and clean the house. Private education and health care are preferred options. Owning a car is still a luxury for many, and *matatus* (privately owned minibuses) are the usual means of travel. Many well-educated Kenyans try to work for

Kenya's country clubs and luxury hotels provide the elite with every comfort and leisure amenity. Such places also create many jobs for much poorer citizens, who may work there as gardeners, porters, cleaners, guards, clerks, and kitchen and bar staff.

While the urban middle classes aspire to European brick villas, the rural poor and nomads still build their homes from brushwood frames sealed with mud and dung. These days, corrugated iron or plastic sheeting makes the roof more watertight.

international companies or aid agencies in Nairobi. The salaries are high, and they may have the opportunity to travel abroad and gain further qualifications.

Rural living

In the countryside, people spend the day collecting water from the stream for washing and cooking, gathering firewood from the bush, and buying corn flour or cooking oil from the nearest market. Children may walk several miles to school after doing household chores. Mothers carry their babies to work in the fields. They also haul heavy loads of water and firewood strung from head straps. Homes are usually rectangular one-story dwellings made of mud brick or wood with iron sheet roofs or thatch. Most homes have no electricity. Earth closets (pit latrines) are the only toilets. Food is cooked on an open fire.

The staple food is corn porridge (*ugali*) or rice in some places. Beans, onions, and kale (*sukuma wiki*) may be added. There are rural *matatus* for transporting heavy produce and bicycle and motorcycle taxis for special trips.

KENYANS TAKING A BREAK

When it comes to time off, urban and rural Kenyans have much in common. They love going to *nyama choma* joints (places that serve barbecued meat). They like chips, soccer, music (from traditional drums to rap, reggae, and gospel), dancing, reading newspapers, television, and radio. Men like drinking beer in pubs. Women like to have their hair done at roadside kiosks or city salons, and there are many church meetings and women's groups to attend. Everywhere, children play with soccer balls made from plastic bags packed tightly inside a net.

Health care

Kenya's health care declined severely after 1992, when the International Monetary Fund (IMF) told the Kenyan government to reduce public spending. This led to serious shortages of medical staff and medicines. Patients now pay for treatment and medical supplies. Sharing beds is common even at Kenyatta National Hospital, once East Africa's flagship hospital. According to the African Medical and Research Foundation (AMREF), a Nairobi-based charity, the government funds only 54 percent of health care. Organizations such as AMREF, together with faith-based missions and traditional healers (*ngangas*), fill the gap.

Death and disease

Malaria and tuberculosis are the main killer diseases. Many children also die from diarrhea caused by waterborne diseases, which are common. Only half the population has access to safe water and sanitation, and many people are malnourished. Around 1 million people have tested positive for the HIV virus, but doctors at Kenyatta National Hospital say type 2 diabetes is the growing crisis as people adopt high-fat, high-sugar Western foods. At least 10 percent of the population (more than 3.7 million) has been diagnosed with this serious condition.

This patient at a rural clinic is lucky to have the bed to himself. In many Kenyan hospitals, overcrowding means that beds must be shared. This problem is often due to discharged patients staying on the wards because they cannot pay their medical bills.

COMPARING COUNTRIES: LIFE EXPECTANCY (IN YEARS)

Country	Male	Female
Japan	79	86
US	75	80
India	62	64
Kenya	52	55
Uganda	49	51
Afghanistan	42	43

Source: World Health Organization, 2008

Medicine men—the *ngangas*

Before the British brought Western medicine to Kenya, every community had a medicine man or woman who was highly respected. Soups made from the leaves and bark of particular trees were used to treat parasitic infections, fevers, and chest and stomach disorders. The *ngangas* still practice today. Scientists have tested some of their remedies and are helping farmers grow medicinal plants to make medications commercially. This improves farmers' income and reduces the need to destroy forest trees and other plants.

Education—the 8-4-4 system

Most children spend at least some years in school and receive a Western-style education. Elementary school lasts eight years and high school and university education four years each. All pupils must study in Kiswahili and English, not in their vernacular language. In 2003, the government's introduction of free elementary education for all increased enrollment, particularly of girls. School fees were a huge burden for most families, and girls were denied in preference to educating boys. This is because girls marry out of the clan, and their education is seen as benefiting another household, whereas boys stay and support their families. High school and higher education must still be paid for, and many students have to find

COMPARING COUNTRIES: LITERACY RATES

Country	Percentage of total population
Cuba	99.8
US	99.0
China	91.9
South Africa	82.4
Kenya	73.6
India	61.0
Bangladesh	47.5
Mali	24.0

Source: United Nations Development Program Report, 2007/2008

sponsorship to continue their education. Many communities must also build their own schools before the government provides teachers. In remote areas of northern Kenya, classes may be held under a large tree with the school library arriving by camel.

High school students must pay or find sponsorship for their education. Elementary school has been free since 2003, resulting in 1 million more children enrolling. This, however, has led to overcrowded classrooms and poor-quality teaching.

CHAPTER 4

Political Changes

During his rule, Moi made Kenya a one-party state, with the Kenya African National Union (KANU) the only legal party. KANU was presented as "the mother and father of the nation," but in reality, the regime was corrupt and repressive. Officials plundered state institutions and took donor funds meant for public services. Opponents were imprisoned and tortured. During the Cold War, Western governments turned a blind eye because Kenya, with its port at Mombasa, was an important ally. But by 1991, when the Soviet Union had crumbled, the US government began to press Moi to reinstate multiparty politics and liberalize the economy. European governments added further pressure by cutting aid budgets.

Hanging on to power

Under pressure from aid cuts, Moi reinstated a multiparty system in time for the 1992 elections. But behind the scenes, his supporters created inter-tribal unrest in the Rift Valley. The main opposition party, Forum for Democracy (FORD), split into factions, which spoiled their chances of defeating Moi. Five years

Violence erupted across Kenya when President Kibaki, a Kikuyu, was declared the 2007 election winner. Odinga's supporters in the Rift Valley vented their fury on all Kikuyus who had settled there, blaming them for the election result.

In 2008, former United Nations (UN) leader Kofi Annan (left) brokered a deal to end the violence after the 2007 elections. Raila Odinga (right) became prime minister, while Kibaki (center) remained president. However, few reforms have taken place.

later, there were still too many opposition parties and Moi won the 1997 elections. The new multiparty constitution, however, then barred him from running in the 2002 elections.

Rainbow victory

Although Moi was forced to retire, he tried to ensure that Uhuru Kenyatta, son of the first president, succeeded him. Finally, the opposition parties united. Mwai Kibaki, a former member of Moi's government and a Kikuyu, led the multi-ethnic National Rainbow Coalition to a resounding victory. He promised Kenyans that he would reform the outdated constitution, reduce presidential powers, and stamp out corruption.

Betrayal

After a referendum on constitutional reform in 2005, it became clear that Kibaki did not intend to reduce his powers or make Kenya a more democratic country. There was no attempt to bring the Moi regime looters to justice, and Moi was appointed as peace envoy to Sudan. At the

2007 election, Raila Odinga, the Luo leader of the Orange Democratic Movement (ODM), was expected to win. His party, with 99 seats in the assembly, represents one of the most populous and under-developed areas of Nyanza, Western Kenya and Rift Valley provinces. When the results showed Kibaki had won, there was widespread violence and accusations of vote rigging.

CASE STUDY: DEADLY POWER GAMES

In the 1990s, Moi clung to power by inciting ethnic conflict in the Rift Valley. He wanted to frighten people from voting for the opposition. After the 2007 elections, political leaders on both sides also orchestrated ethnic violence. Over 1,000 people were killed, and 350,000 were chased from their farms and businesses. Kikuyus who had settled outside their traditional tribal area were the main victims. The Luo and Kalenjin ODM supporters blamed them for Kibaki's victory. Some believed that the Kikuyu had more than their fair share of land after independence—a grudge that politicians continue to manipulate.

Majimbo—another way to govern Kenya?

When Kenya first gained independence, some opposition leaders thought that a federation, or *majimbo*, where regions governed their own affairs, would be the best system. But Kenyatta believed a centralized government made Kenya stronger. In recent times, ODM leader Raila Odinga and many coastal members of parliament have again been calling for *majimbo*, saying it is a fairer way to rule Kenya. President Kibaki and other leaders do not like this option.

Kenya's laws are made in the one-house National Assembly, also known as parliament or *bunge*. Bills passed there become acts of parliament only on the president's say-so. Kenyans have long been calling for the reduction of such presidential power.

Lawmakers—The National Assembly

Kenya's National Assembly has 210 elected members and 12 nominated by the president to represent special interests. Everyone over age 18 has a vote, and elections take place every five years. The president is head of state and commander in chief of the armed forces. There is a vice president, and since 2008, the post of prime minister has been created as part of the Grand Coalition between the main parties ODM and the Party of National Unity (PNU). Proceedings are transcribed as in the British parliamentary system. The attorney general is the government's principal legal adviser.

The constitution

In 1963, at independence, the constitution was drawn up. Based on the colonial model, where an unelected governor had authoritarian powers, it is not suited to multiparty democracy. President Kibaki's powers are still considerable. In 2000, the Constitution of Kenya Review Commission started collecting people's views and found that most wanted presidential powers reduced to prevent abuse. In 2004, the Kenyan government agreed to create the post of prime minister and drew up the Bomas Draft. But this power-sharing reform was only implemented in 2008 under pressure from Kofi Annan. In 2009, he was still urging the leaders to make the political reforms that Kenyans want.

Justice

Kenyan and English statute law provide the main legal framework, but there is also customary (tribal) law and Islamic law. In family disputes, such as quarrels over where a deceased person is to be buried, all forms might be consulted. Courts include the Court of Appeal, the High Court, resident and district magistrates' courts, and *kadhis* courts, which rule on Muslim family matters. The judiciary is constitutionally independent, but the president appoints the judges, who have tenure until they reach the age of 74. In 2003, the anti-corruption authority found proof that half of the High Court judges and a third of magistrates had abused their position. Many judges were suspended and then resigned rather than face tribunals. But by 2009, further reform of the judiciary had stalled.

The Kenyan flag was adopted in December 1963. It is based on the black, red, and green colors of the KANU flag, the party that led to Kenya's independence.

FOCUS: THE KENYAN FLAG

The symbolism behind the Kenyan flag

Black represents the people of Kenya.

Red represents the struggle for freedom.

Green represents Kenya's agriculture and natural resources.

White represents unity and peace.

The Masai shield and spears represent the defense of each element represented in the flag.

Public order

The Kenyan police force has about 35,000 officers, mostly in urban areas. This includes a criminal investigation department, which since 2001 also has an anti-corruption unit. Provincial administrators have their own police force. The national parks are protected from poachers by the Kenya Wildlife Service, and the nation's security is maintained by an army, navy, and air force.

Civil rights movements

There are many Kenyan social justice groups. The Federation of Women Lawyers (FIDA) works to end discrimination against women. The Green Belt Movement (see page 42) plants trees to

(see page 42)

FOCUS: CORRUPTION AND ABUSE OF POWER

Kenya's corrupt officials are costing the nation around $1.6 billion per year. Even the poorest citizens report paying up to 16 bribes a month. The police, in particular, make up low pay by threatening citizens with arrest if they do not pay a bribe.

combat soil erosion and improve women farmers' livelihoods. The Oscar Foundation provides a free legal aid clinic for thousands of poor people. The Kenya National Commission on Human Rights gathers evidence of police and government abuses. In a 2009 press release, Professor Wangari Maathai, founder of the Green Belt Movement and 2004 Nobel Peace Prize laureate, said human rights activists still risked police intimidation, arrest, and death and urged Kenyans to stand by them.

Mungiki—gangsters or dissidents?

Since the 1980s, a group called the Mungiki Sect has grown up in Nairobi and Central Province. Mostly young Kikuyu men, they originally modeled themselves on Mau Mau freedom fighters but in recent times have been accused of extortion and gangster tactics. In 2002, a special police squad was appointed to deal with them. In 2009, a United Nations investigator visited Kenya to research claims by civil rights groups that the police were guilty of extra-judicial killings of alleged

Professor Wangari Maathai won the 2004 Nobel Peace Prize for her tireless efforts to replant Kenya's threatened forests and improve farm women's lives. During the Moi era, she braved imprisonment and death threats for this cause.

Mungiki members. He concluded that Kenya's police killed at will and called for the resignation of the chief of police and the attorney general. Officials deny the accusations.

Nairobi police arrest a suspected Mungiki Sect member in April 2008. Mungiki clashed with police after the murder of their leader's wife.

COMPARING COUNTRIES— CORRUPTION RATES

Out of 180 countries, the following were ranked:

New Zealand, Sweden, Denmark	9.3	(least corrupt)	1st
UK, Ireland	7.7		16th
US	7.3		18th
Italy	4.8		55th
Indonesia, Libya, Uganda	2.6		126th
Kenya, Syria, Russia	2.1		147th
Somalia	1	(most corrupt)	180th

Source: Transparency International Corruption Index 2008

Media

Kenya's state-owned Kenya Broadcasting Corporation is the only broadcaster that covers the nation. Since liberalization in 1991, private radio and TV stations have sprung up, but their range is mostly limited to Nairobi. Kenya has a lively press, including world-class English language newspapers, the *Daily Nation* and *Standard*, which can also be read on the Internet. Under Kibaki, there has been greater editorial independence, but journalists investigating government wrongdoing may still suffer police intimidation. The Internet, though, now lets Kenyans air their views in ways that were unthinkable under the Moi regime.

CHAPTER 5

Economic and Environmental Changes

Kenya is the financial and communications center of East Africa. It has a free market economy and an active stock exchange. Kenyan-Asian entrepreneurs who dominate the business and manufacturing scene have international connections. Multinational companies own plantations of tea, flowers, coffee, pineapples, and tobacco. They have shares in international tourism, information technology, cell phones, oil,

banking, and power production. International donors including the US, Germany, and the UK have invested heavily in improving infrastructure, training, and agriculture. The port, airports,

Tea is Kenya's main export earner after cut flowers and tourism. It grows on large estates and small farms in the cool highlands of Central and Western provinces. Climate change due to destruction of the Mau Forest is now threatening this industry.

railway, and major highways provide regional and international connections. Kenya belongs to the East African Community with Tanzania and Uganda and is a member of the Common Market for East and Southern Africa (COMESA). It has a highly educated workforce and a hardworking underclass. In 2009, to boost regional trade, an undersea cable between the United Arab Emirates and Mombasa was laid. It will make Internet access quicker and cheaper.

Economic reality

During the Moi years, economic growth was poor, but when Kibaki came to power in 2003, he launched the Economic Recovery Strategy. By 2007, the Kenya Bureau of Statistics recorded a gross domestic product of $29,509,000, a rise of over 5 percent. Even so, Kenya is prone to boom and bust years. Ten years of drought and a dependence on rain-fed crops threaten the country's mainstay—agriculture. Coverage of the post-election violence in 2008 seriously affected

FOCUS: KENYA'S TOP EARNERS 2007

	$	
Tourism	1 billion	1 million visitors
Flowers	616 million	100,100 tons
Tea	537 million	421,740 tons
Coffee	142 million	59,400 tons

Sources: The *Guardian*, Kenya Flower Council, TradeInvest Kenya, Kenya Coffee Board

the tourist market, another major foreign currency earner. Corruption, dependence on aid and World Bank loans, servicing an international debt, and failure to restore infrastructure, including roads that link local people to markets, all hamper potential growth, which has dropped to 2 percent.

Failure to industrialize

Most Kenyans are farmers at heart. Fewer than 2 million of 37 million people are in full-time waged employment, and of these, most are government employees or service industry workers. Large-scale agricultural production includes tea, coffee, green beans, and flowers, but Kenya's industrial base is small. While small-scale consumer products such as cigarettes, textiles, batteries, soap, and plastic goods are made, most manufactured products are imported, amounting to twice the value of the country's exports. Three-quarters of the population still depend on owning some land or cattle for their livelihood. Most are subsistence farmers, although around 25,000 small farmers also contribute to important horticulture exports by growing luxury crops such as green beans and sugar peas for Western supermarkets.

While tourism and agricultural exports earn $4.7 billion per year, manufactured imports cost Kenya $9.5 billion. Kenya thus needs to industrialize if it is to develop. In the meantime, it is the farm wives selling their surplus at market who feed the nation.

GDP composition by industry

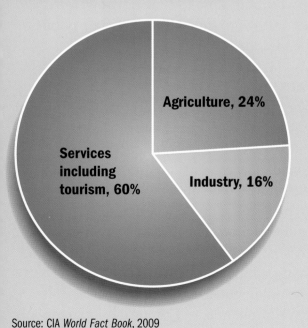

Agriculture, 24%

Services including tourism, 60%

Industry, 16%

Source: CIA *World Fact Book*, 2009

People power

Kenya's hardworking people are the backbone of the economy. Besides farming, many run small businesses. With no social services and pensions, everyone must find some way to make a living.

Jua kali—the "fierce sun" workers

Every roadside has its street artisans—mechanics, woodworkers, barbers, dressmakers. They are called *jua kali* because they work under the hot sun. Shoppers can bargain for beds, sofa sets, chicken feeders, garden plants, and so on. Every locality also has kiosks. Some sell African tourist curios, others sell fizzy drinks, but most sell essentials such as corn flour, milk, tea, soap, salt, cigarettes, cooking oil, kerosene for lamps, charcoal for stoves, headache pills, and Vaseline skin salve. Owners split packages into smaller quantities to make goods more affordable—customers can buy one cigarette or two aspirins. These informal traders pay licenses to operate but are still vulnerable to town council demolition

Small roadside stores and kiosks serve the needs of millions of ordinary people. They sell everything from milk, fresh vegetables, and aspirin to kerosene, live chickens, and sofas. They provide cell phone repairs, car parts, tailoring, and haircuts.

squads, who from time to time destroy their premises on the grounds of their being a public nuisance or unpaid licenses.

Markets

These are the heart of Kenya's economic life, from sea- or lakeside fish markets, to the big produce markets of Nairobi, to car parts and secondhand clothes markets. *Mitumba*, European cast-off clothes, come in container loads to Kenya. Their popularity has undermined local clothing production, but Kenyans say they prefer the quality of secondhand designer goods. Rural areas have trading centers—usually a row of stores including general goods, hardware, butchers, and pharmacy. The local buses stop outside, so there are also bars, tea kiosks, and an

CASE STUDY: UPWARDLY MOBILE

Kenya's telephone landlines are expensive and often do not work. Cell phones have revolutionized people's lives. Repair shops have mushroomed and kiosks hire out phones. Farmers use them to check produce prices and cut out the middlemen. Traders without bank accounts can send money home by phone at transfer kiosks, which saves lining up at post offices to send money orders that are often stolen. This revolutionary service was first developed in Kenya by Safaricom and Vodafone. Kenya has 80 percent cell phone coverage, including the remote Rift Valley, where Maasai elders now use solar-charged cells to check on their cattle.

open-air market where farmers' wives sell surplus bananas, tomatoes, spinach, beans, and onions. However, women earn little from this trade because they are competing with many neighbors selling the same produce.

Transportation

Bad roads hamper all farm trade in Kenya. Small farmers without a vehicle are prey to middlemen, who come to their farms and set the lowest prices. But transportation difficulties also generate small businesses. Besides the *matatu* owners, who transport people, animals, and goods, there are bicycle taxis called *boda boda* and handcart and donkey cart owners who hire out their haulage services. In recent times, the government has given loans to unemployed youths to set up motorcycle taxis that are now taking over from bicycles in many rural areas.

Cell phones have revolutionized Kenyans' lives, from Maasai cattle owners who use them to keep in touch with their herdsmen to city traders checking on commodity prices. The M-Pesa service for using phones to transfer money was pioneered in Kenya.

Deforestation

Nearly three-quarters of Kenya's household energy comes from wood. Many people make a living by burning timber to make charcoal for sale in the towns. Over time, the loss of forest cover reduces cloud formation, making the local climate increasingly dry. Without deep tree roots that tap into underground water sources, streams dry up. Then soil blows away during periods of drought or creates landslides during heavy rainstorms. So begins a downward spiral of poverty, for both the people and their land.

A Rendille girl gathers cooking fuel for her family. Across the country, women spend many hours a day finding firewood. This time could be spent more productively in the fields, looking after children, or at market.

Sources of Kenya's energy

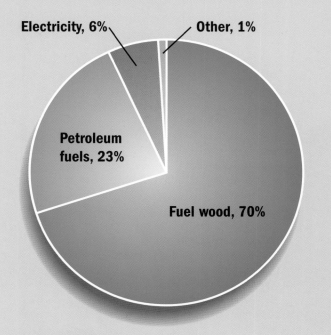

Electricity, 6%

Other, 1%

Petroleum fuels, 23%

Fuel wood, 70%

Source: *Kenya: Atlas of Our Changing Environment*
United Nations Environment Program, 2009

Power struggle

Most electricity in Kenya is generated by hydroelectric power, together with some geothermal power (using the Rift Valley steam vents) and oil-fueled production. Yet this electricity only meets about one-fifth of the nation's power needs, and lack of power means that most industry is concentrated in urban areas. Power is extremely costly for consumers and is subject to frequent rationing when drought affects the hydropower dams. Many industries have relocated to other countries because of these factors.

Hydropower and some geothermal power provide most of the country's electricity, although few rural areas have a supply. There is an overdependency on wood for fuel, which depletes the soil and makes the climate drier.

Poverty trap

The majority of rural dwellers and slum dwellers live without electricity. They rely on kerosene to light lamps, diesel to power small mills to grind corn, and wood or charcoal for their cooking. The destruction of forests that feed river systems also threatens both large- and small-scale hydropower projects. At independence, 12 percent of available Kenyan land was forested; now the surviving 1.7 percent is under increasing threat from logging and subsistence farmers wanting more farmland.

Population growth

As this farmland becomes more impoverished and prone to drought, so the demands on it by the growing population increase. Despite the fact that at least 9 million out of 37 million Kenyans live on less than a dollar a day, the population continues to rise. It is nearly four times greater than it was at independence. With more than half the population (53 percent) under 20 years old, this also puts a great strain on family budgets.

Mass tourism: costs and benefits

Although mass tourism is Kenya's major income earner and the hotels and safari lodges provide jobs for local people, it also has serious costs. On the one hand, tourists provide revenue to fund conservation and the wildlife service. Their demand for wildlife experiences gives Kenyans a reason to protect wildlife that they might otherwise destroy because it conflicts with their farming needs. But mass tourism also creates environmental problems. The luxury safari lodges are within game reserves. High-consuming Westerners create large amounts of sewage and trash that is usually buried or burned near the lodges. The tour buses that take visitors on game-viewing drives over grassland cause pollution and disrupt animal feeding and breeding patterns. Tourists encourage the drug and sex trade. In recent times, there have been moves to develop small-scale, high-value ecotourism. Foreign tourists are guided through the bush by the Maasai, and every effort is made to minimize tourism's negative effects on the environment.

The Laikipia District is a vast plateau northwest of Mount Kenya, in the Rift Valley Province. Here, deep gorges show the grim effects of soil erosion.

CHAPTER 6

Changing Relationships

Kenya's relations with the international community are dominated by accusations of official corruption and lawlessness. While President Obama points out that corruption is a vice found in all societies, in 2009, he told the Kenyan government that if it wants further financial assistance from the US and elsewhere, the corruption must stop and reform must begin.

Barack Obama sets the agenda

In 2006, when Senator Obama visited Kenya, he had some blunt words for Nairobi University students. He said there must be an end to ethnic-based politics that channeled the nation's wealth to favored family groups or tribes at the expense of the public good. It was up to them, he challenged students, to determine how their nation would progress in the twenty-first century, "whether the hard work of the many is lost to the selfish desires of the few or whether you build an open, honest, stronger Kenya where everyone rises together."

International debt

Kenya has relied on loans from foreign governments since independence, when the British government loaned President Kenyatta $19 million to buy farms from departing European settlers. The interest that accrues on such loans eats into national budgets. Indebted governments then seek more loans to pay for

In 2006, Senator Barack Obama visited Kenya, his father's homeland. Here, he is greeting supporters at the memorial site of the 1998 bombing of the US embassy in Nairobi. Kenyans are very proud that "a son of Kenya" has become president of the US.

Gabbra women collect food aid after losing their herds to drought. In 2009, the Kenyan government declared itself powerless to help 10 million drought-stricken Kenyans. Instead, ordinary people raised $2.4 million to fund the Mercy Train, which delivered emergency food to starving people.

essential services. Many Kenyan human rights workers such as Wangari Maathai believe that World Bank loans have only enriched corrupt officials and left ordinary Kenyans worse off, both in debt and without the services the loans were supposed to pay for. By 2007, Kenya's international debt was nearly $7 billion, with annual servicing costs of $248 million. In April 2009, the Kenyan government asked the International Monetary Fund for more money so it could pay for the costs of running its free elementary school program.

International aid

Foreign aid has become a way of life in Kenya. Nairobi is the base for international development agencies and local nongovernmental organizations. Church missions also run development projects and government agencies such as the US USAID and UK DFID fund projects throughout the country. In 2000, at the UN Millennium Summit, 189 nations, including Kenya, voted to support eight Millennium Development Goals (MDG) to relieve the world's poorest nations. Aid projects now aim to meet these targets by 2015. However, in 2008, Kenya's minister for development reported that Kenya was only likely to meet the elementary school education and disease targets. He blamed lack of funds from developed nations. The MDG steering group also stated that climate change was jeopardizing these goals in African countries.

FOCUS: MILLENNIUM DEVELOPMENT GOALS (MDGs) FOR THE WORLD'S POOREST COUNTRIES BY 2015

- Halving extreme poverty and hunger
- Achieving universal elementary school education
- Promoting equality between men and women
- Reducing under-age-five child deaths by two-thirds
- Reducing deaths of mothers giving birth by three-quarters
- Reversing spread of HIV/AIDS, malaria, and TB
- Ensuring environmental sustainability
- Developing a global development partnership with aid, trade, and debt relief targets

Global warming and climate change

Although Kenya's carbon emissions are low, the country is now suffering from the effects of climate change caused by emissions from wealthy countries. Reduced rainfall in the tea-growing area west of Mau Forest is already causing a downturn

Climate change is the greatest threat to people who live in arid areas. Wajir, in North Eastern Province, is becoming increasingly drought ridden. For Kenya's Somali herders who live there, dead cattle means their families may also die.

in tea production, Kenya's major export earner. Increased aridity of the east and north and the continued failure of rains across the rest of the country also caused the 2009 famine, which is affecting nearly one-quarter of the population. In the highlands, the warmer climate is increasing the incidence of malaria where it rarely occurred before and where people have little resistance.

Banking crisis

The global recession is affecting earnings from important exports such as flowers. Western consumers are cutting back on such luxuries, but this means one-third of Kenyan flower workers may be facing job losses. Tourism is another key

COMPARING COUNTRIES: CO_2 EMISSIONS IN BILLION TONS

Country	1990	2004
US	5.3	6.7
China	2.6	5.5
South Africa	0.4	0.5
Kenya	0.006	0.01
Mali	0.0004	0.0007

CO_2 emissions in tons per capita
Kenya, 0.3; US, 22.7; China, 4.2

Source: United Nations Development Program, 2007/2008

FOCUS: KENYA'S BRAIN DRAIN

Kenya is a major exporter of doctors, nurses, and teachers. They leave for better-paid jobs and living conditions in the US, UK, Australia, and other parts of Africa. This skills loss is a huge setback to Kenya's welfare and development. From 2001 to 2006, 3,390 nurses left Kenya for jobs in the US, UK, Australia, and New Zealand. In Nairobi's Kenyatta Hospital, there are 1,800 beds with three nurses to every 80 patients. Nurses earn less than $264 per month but can earn 10 times more than this abroad.

Source: The Body, US Centers for Disease Control and Prevention International News, 2006

Relations with Britain

A former colonial power, the UK still has many business interests in Kenya. There are more than 60 UK firms in Kenya, with a combined estimated worth of $2.4 billion. Kenya imports $310 million worth of British goods and exports $505 million in return. The descendants of some British white settlers still live there, and the UK is one of Kenya's major donors, supporting education and HIV/AIDS health programs with a 2008–2009 budget of $80 million.

threatened area. Visitor figures may be expected to fall as Europeans decide to stay home. Other important income from Kenyans who work abroad and send money home has also shrunk.

Bad neighbors

Kenya's northeast borders are impossible to control, and this leads to security problems. Neighboring Somalia is deemed to be a failed state. Somali bandits armed with AK-47s threaten the Turkana and Samburu nomads. Weapons also find their way into Kenya's criminal sector. There are fears, too, that Somali extremists will target Kenya due to the government's cooperation with the US on terrorism. In 1998, Kenya's US embassy was bombed by the Egyptian Islamic Jihad, killing 200 Kenyans and injuring 4,000 others. Recently, Kenya and the US have formed a partnership to stop terrorism at the ports.

Since 1992, the refugee camp at Liboi, just inside the Kenyan border, has received hundreds of thousands of Somali refugees, fleeing their country's civil war. Other refugee camps such as Dadaab are also massively overcrowded.

CHAPTER 7

Future Challenges

In 2009, the Grand Coalition continued to work to reform the constitution. Many Kenyans still suffer the effects of post-election violence, and thousands are displaced. Millions rely on food aid due to conflict or famine. The government is in debt and depends on loans and aid to run its departments. Mungiki members and the police are terrorizing the public. There can be no lasting development until government corruption is stopped and wrongdoers are brought to justice. Kenya must also replant its forests to combat the effects of local and global climate change. Yet despite all the problems, many Kenyans are working hard to transform people's lives.

CASE STUDY: COMBATTING CLIMATE CHANGE AND POVERTY

Wangari Maathai's Green Belt Movement (see page 30) has so far mobilized 100,000 women to plant 3 million trees in an attempt to reverse local climate changes. Now the UN Environment Program has adopted her scheme globally. With fellow patron Prince Albert of Monaco, Maathai is overseeing the Billion Tree Campaign. Already 3 billion trees have been planted worldwide, with a 7 billion target set for the end of 2009. So far, Ethiopia has planted the most trees (725 million), while Turkey comes in second with 7 million. Wangari says, "When we plant trees, we plant the seeds of peace and seeds of hope."

The Green Belt Movement is replanting native trees to feed the soil. Some species can be grown as living fences that protect fields from wild game while being cropped for firewood, medicines, and animal fodder.

Empowering rural production

Simon Mwacharo Guyo of www.craftskills.biz has developed a range of low-cost wind turbines that he calls "wind cruisers." They provide farms, rural schools, clinics, and workshops with clean electricity. In the highlands, micro-hydro projects run by local people are harnessing the power from small rivers to bring clean, renewable power to many village homes. These low-technology systems are improving people's lives and making their businesses more efficient.

Harvests from dry land

For six years, Isaac Kalua, founder of the Green Africa Foundation, has been growing oil-rich *jatropha curcas* bushes in the driest areas of Kitui, Eastern Province, where little else will grow. The seeds can be ground using simple milling technology to make clean bio-diesel and lamp oil. One acre (0.4 hectare) of otherwise unproductive land can earn about $1,200 a year (twice as much from a similar plot of tea) and so help to lift people out of poverty.

Healing ethnic conflict

Tegla Loroupe, Kenya's world champion female marathon runner, has set up the Tegla Loroupe Peace Foundation. Its aim is to bring peace through sports to conflict zones in East Africa. Besides organizing athletics races for young Rift Valley warriors, the foundation is building a school for 400 orphaned or displaced students.

Kenya's future rests on the skills of its resourceful people. They have waited a long time for their government to deliver true independence. But in the meantime, visitors to Kenya can be sure to be met with great generosity. The word they will most often hear is *karibu*—"welcome, come on in."

Samuel Kamau Wansiru celebrates winning the men's marathon at the Beijing 2008 Olympic Games. Kenya produces many world-class runners. Some athletes joke that this is because they grew up chasing cattle!

Timeline

1895 Formation of the British East African Protectorate; building of the Mombasa to Uganda railway begins.

1920 British East African Protectorate becomes Kenya Crown Colony.

1944 Kenya African Union (KANU) is formed to campaign for African rights.

1952 Kikuyu uprising starts with a campaign against loyalist chiefs. A state of emergency is called.

1953 Kenyatta is found guilty of masterminding the Mau Mau uprising in a rigged trial and is detained.

1960 State of emergency ends.

1961 Kenyatta is released from detention and becomes president of KANU, formed by Tom Mboya and Oginga Odinga.

1963 Kenya gains independence with Jomo Kenyatta, a Kikuyu, as prime minister.

1964 Republic of Kenya is formed. Kenyatta is Kenya's first president, with Oginga Odinga as vice president.

1978 President Kenyatta dies and is succeeded by a Kalenjin, Daniel arap Moi.

1982 Failed coup attempt by the Kenya air force to oust Moi.

1991 After suspension of Western aid, Moi announces multiparty elections.

1992 First multiparty elections are preceded by ethnic violence in the Rift Valley. The Kalenjins, the president's tribe, target all non-Kalenjins to stop opposition voters.

1997 Daniel arap Moi wins the election as opposition parties fail to unite. This follows orchestrated ethnic conflict in the Rift Valley and at the coast.

Aug. 1998 Bombing of US embassy in Nairobi.

Sept. 2000 UN Millennium Summit of 189 countries in New York establishes eight Millennium Development Goals. Kenya is a signatory.

Dec. 2002 President Moi is replaced by Mwai Kibaki, heading the National Rainbow Coalition of opposition parties.

Mar. 2004 Bomas Draft agreement for reform, including reduction of presidential powers.

Nov. 2005 Referendum on constitutional reform; Kenyans reject the Kibaki draft.

Oct. 2006 Kenyan government launches Kenya Vision 2030, its target for a democratic, middle-income nation.

Dec. 2007 General election. President Kibaki stands for a second term, but Raila Odinga, head of ODM, is expected to win.

Jan. 2008 Post-election violence in which ODM supporters target Kikuyus, blaming them for Kibaki's win.

Feb. 2008 Former UN leader Kofi Annan brokers the Grand Coalition between President Kibaki and Raila Odinga, who is made prime minister.

Feb. 2009 UN investigator calls for resignation of attorney general and chief of police over police extra-judicial killings of Mungiki suspects.

Apr. 2009 Prime Minister Raila Odinga says power-sharing deal is not working and calls for new elections.

Glossary

arable Land that is suitable for growing crops.

askari Kiswahili word used in colonial times for an African policeman and soldier; now used in original meaning for a guard.

autocratic System of government ruled by one person, a despot.

Bantu A group of African people who speak one of 500 related languages.

clan Group of people related by blood, descended from a common ancestor.

Cushite Group of languages and their speakers from Ethiopia and Somalia.

coalition Union of groups sharing a political or military purpose.

Crown Colony A British colony controlled by the British Crown, represented by a governor.

dhow Arab sailing ship with a triangular (lateen) sail.

escarpment Long, steep cliff at the edge of a plateau.

extended family A single family and all its blood relatives.

gross domestic product (GDP) Total market value of products and services produced by a country.

harambee A Kiswahili word meaning "All pull together." KANU slogan.

hominid Extinct human-like human ancestors.

International Monetary Fund (IMF) The IMF was set up by the UN in 1944 to aid trade by stabilizing currency exchange rates.

KANU Kenya African National Union. The ruling party after independence.

Kiswahili The language of the coastal Swahili people, a fusion of Bantu and Arabic.

majimbo A term coined at independence meaning a federal system of government.

monsoon Seasonal wind in South Asia that brings rain.

Nongovernmental organizations (NGOs) Agencies that work in development, such as Oxfam or Water Aid.

Nilotic Refers to a group of language speakers who originated in the Nile basin, including Maasai and Luo peoples.

nomadic Not living in one place.

nuclear family Basic family unit comprising mother, father, and children.

Orange Democratic Movement (ODM) A group headed by Raila Odinga.

paleontology The study of fossils.

PNU Party of National Unity, headed by President Mwai Kibaki.

polygamy Family where the husband has more than one wife at the same time.

protectorate A territory controlled but not owned by a stronger state.

soldier-settler scheme A British government scheme to give British service veterans cheap land to farm in Kenya.

state of emergency A period during which government suspends everyday life, often with the loss of civil liberties.

segregation A limitation of people's freedom of movement and access to services based on race.

tribe A group of several clans who all claim a common, if distant, ancestor.

uhuru Kiswahili word meaning "freedom" or "independence."

vernacular One's native language or mother tongue.

World Bank Set up by the UN at Bretton Woods in 1944 to help developing countries with loans.

Further information

Websites

www.greenafricafoundation.org/default.asp
Growing bio-diesel in arid eastern Kenya.

www.wri.org/publications/content/9373
Atlas of Ecosystems and Human Well-Being— Kenya, World Resources Institute, 2007.

www.cia.gov/library/publications/the-world-factbook/geos/ke.html
CIA, *The World Factbook, Kenya*

www.dfid.gov.uk/countries/africa/kenya.asp
Britain's Department for International Development's Kenya page; downloadable reports and fact sheets, information on aid projects, general country facts and figures.

www.unep.org/dewa/africa/kenyaatlas/PDF/Kenya_Atlas_Full_EN_72dpi.pdf
Kenya: Atlas of our Changing Environment 2009 UN Environment Program.

www.usaid.gov/ke/
US International Development Kenya page.

Books

Cantwell, Rebecca. *Teens in Kenya.* Compass Point Books US, 2005.

Kenyatta, Jomo. *Facing Mount Kenya.* Vintage Books 1962. Anthropology of the Kikuyu by Kenya's first president, first published in 1932.

Kenya Travel Guide, 7th ed. Lonely Planet, 2009.

Maathai, Wangari. *Unbowed: One Woman's Story.* Heinemann, 2007. Autobiography of Kenya's best known human rights and environmental campaigner, 2004 Nobel Peace Prize laureate. She explains Kenya's last 60 years in light of her own struggles.

For African nonfiction and fiction books (including Kenya) by African writers, see the African Books Collective website:
http://africanbookscollective.com
PO Box 721, Oxford, OX1 9EN UK

Index

Page numbers in **bold** refer to illustrations and charts.